Animal Mandalas for Colouring

David Benham

Animal Mandalas for Colouring

ISBN-10: 1503366499
ISBN-13: 978-1503366497

www.davidbenham.co.uk

Colouring is fun, whatever your age.

These decorative mandalas have been designed to provide hours of relaxing enjoyment
with their repeated shapes and intricate patterns.
They can be coloured however you choose.

In this collection you'll find the following animals:

Owl	Elephant	Horse
Dog	Dragonfly	Bat
Chameleon	Monkey	Spider
Hummingbird	Frog	Lion
Bear	Parrot	Dolphin
Turtle	Squirrel	Chicken
Peacock	Beetle	Seahorse
Giraffe	Tiger	Snake
Crocodile	Octopus	Tropical Fish
Butterfly	Crab	Cat

The back of each colouring page is blank so that when your own
unique work of art is finished, it can be cut out and hung up for display.

So grab those pens or pencils and dive in...

13108526R00037

Printed in Great Britain
by Amazon.co.uk, Ltd.,
Marston Gate.